The Crochet Wildlife Guide

For videos and more, visit

crochetwildlifeguide.com

First Printing, 2016

ISBN 978-0-9958060-2-3

1 - 1608 16 Avenue SW
Calgary, Alberta, T3C 1A1

www.crochetwildlifeguide.com
info@crochetwildlifeguide.com

Table of contents

Patterns

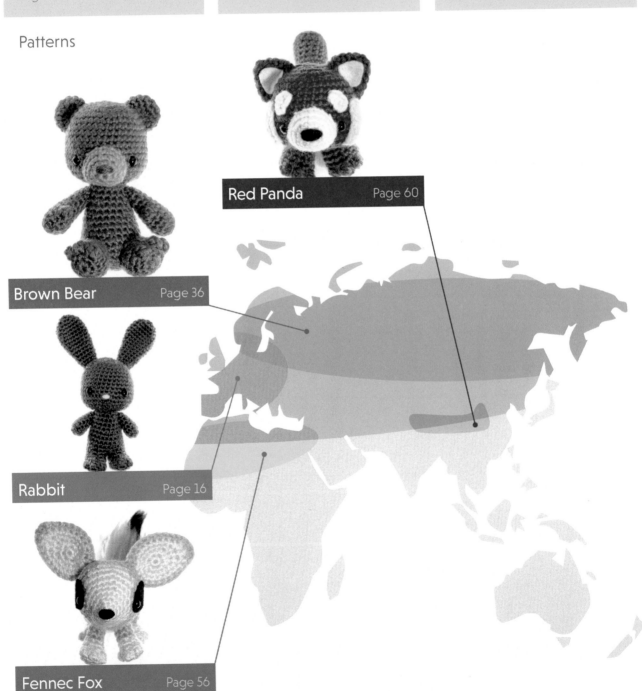

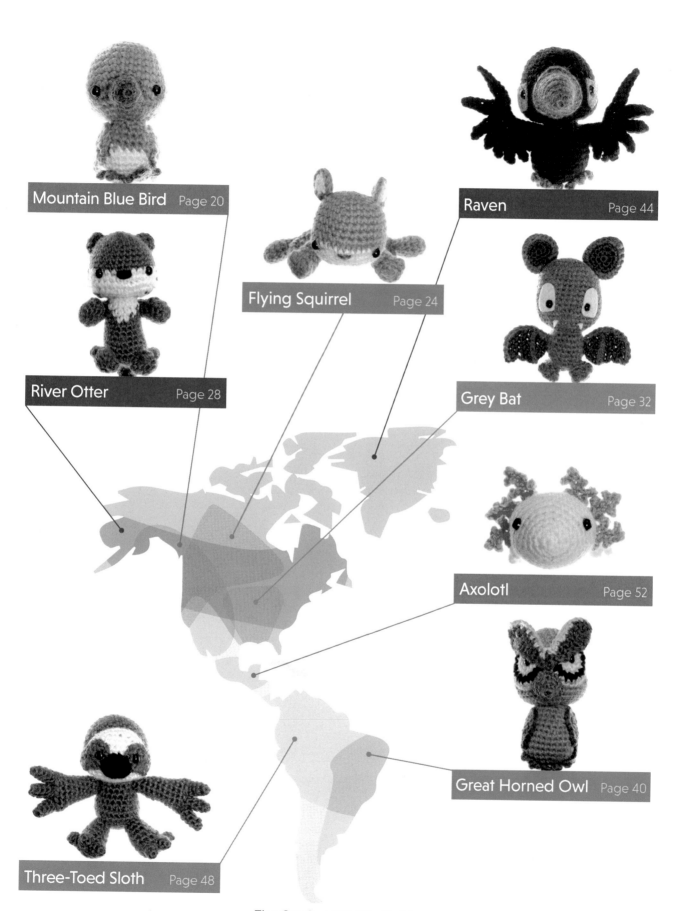

Crochet inspired by wildlife

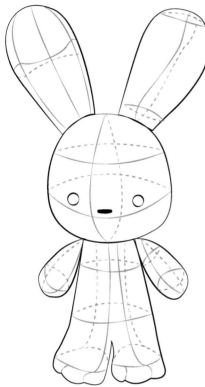

The animal world is far from boring.

Animals come in all shapes, sizes and colors. Even the most similar species have traits that make them completely different.

Crocheting is the perfect way to explore the diverse world of animals. With just a hook and yarn, endless shapes can be created.

At its most basic, the craft of crocheting is simple. It is the process of looping yarn into interlocking knots to form chains, and then creating swatches by adding more rows of loops onto the chain. And all this is done with just one tool – a humble crochet hook.

Even 3D shapes – from spheres to bizarre blobs – are possible with a crochet hook. This is done in a manner similar to a 3D printer, by building the object from the bottom to the top (or the top to the bottom). Objects are then stuffed to help them keep their shape.

The art of creating 3D stuffed animals or dolls by crocheting is called amigurumi. While also possible with knitting, it is more common for amigurumi projects to be done by crocheting.

All patterns in *The Crochet Wildlife Guide* are based off of real-life species from around the world. There is the adorable red panda from the Himalayas, the peculiar axolotl from Central America, the cuddly

The word *crochet* means *small hook* in French

brown bear from North America and many more. The patterns reflect the animals' unique shapes, while keeping amigurumi's signature cuteness.

For new crocheters and those needing a little refresher on techniques and stitches, the first section of the book contains all the necessary tools and tips to begin amigurumi. The patterns come in three difficulties, and the illustrations will help guide the way through more complex procedures.

Creativity is important in amigurumi. Experiment with different yarns,

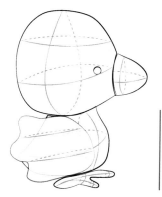

> *Amigurumi* is Japanese, from *ami* (meaning crocheted or knitted) and *nuigurumi* (meaning stuffed doll or animal)

"Let Nature be your teacher"
William Wordsworth, 1798

hook sizes and colors to create animals or creatures from a totally different world. A great way to begin creating unique animals is mix-and-matching pieces from various patterns throughout the book.

Yarn colors are only suggestions, and some pleasant yarn alternatives are pictured in a few patterns. Acrylic yarn has been used in all the photos, but natural yarns can make softer and cuddlier creatures.

Personal tension and crochet styles will create unique end results – even when using the same pattern and yarn. And that is alright!

Animals of the same species can look very different, so it is natural if the final result is not what was initially intended. Your new creation may just be a newly discovered species.

How to use this book

Following a pattern

Most amigurumi pieces start with a magic loop – a yarn ring that holds stitches together in a circle. From there, stitches are added on in spirals to form spheres, cones or random shapes. Other amigurumi pieces are started with a foundation chain and end up as flat pieces. Pieces are stuffed with stuffing (or anything else) and then sewn together with yarn. Extras – such as safety eyes and felt swatches – add special touches that yarn just can't do.

Patterns use metric measurements and USA crochet abbreviations.

Rounds and rows

Rounds and rows are the two main arrangements of stitches. Rounds (a) are worked in one direction using continuous circles. Rows (b) are worked back-and-forth, often using chain stitches to go from one row to another and turning the piece after every row. In amigurumi, rounds are more often used because the stitches all look identical. Rows have more visible stripes that are formed from turning the piece after every row.

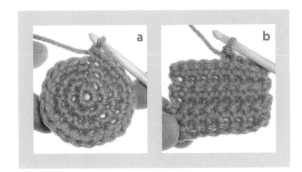

Pattern overview

	Rabbit	Mountain Bluebird	Flying Squirrel	River Otter	Grey Bat	Brown Bear	Great Horned Owl	Raven	Three-Toed Sloth	Axolotl	Fennec Fox	Red Panda
Skill level	●○○	●○○	●●●	●○○	●●○	●○○	●●○	●●○	●●○	●●●	●●●	●●○
Single crochet	●	●	●	●	●	●	●	●	●	●	●	●
Double crochet							●			●		
Half double crochet		●	●	●		●	●			●		●
Yarn color changes		●	●	●			●			●		
Puff stitch	●		●	●	●				●			
Latch hook stitch										●		
Felt			●	●			●					
Safety eyes	●	●	●	●	●	●	●	●	●	●	●	●
Brushed yarn											●	
Page number	16	20	24	28	32	36	40	44	48	52	56	60

R1 Round and row number

For parts that are made in one row (such as bird's feet), the steps are numbered without "R." Unless otherwise noted, pieces are made in rounds.

(6) Stitch number

The total number of stitches in each row or round. Useful to double check accuracy and visualize the overall changes in shape as stitches are added or removed.

(A) Yarn color

Suggested yarn colors for the pattern. Within the pattern, capital letters indicate which yarn color to use for each part.

Fennec Fox

Vulpes zerda

Yarn Colors
Brown (A)
Cream (B)
Black (C)

Notions
2 safety eyes
Stuffing
Black felt

Measurements
11 cm
6 cm
20 cm

Skill Level ●●●

Head

R1	With B, sc 6 in magic ring (6)
R2	(sc 1, inc) three times (9)
R3	(sc 2, inc) three times (12)
R4	(sc 1, inc) six times (18)
R5	sc in each st around (18)
R6	(sc 2, inc) six times (24)
R7	Switch to A, (sc 3, inc) two times, switch to B, (sc 3, inc) two times, switch to A, (sc 3, inc) two times (30)
R8	(sc 4, inc) two times, switch to B, (sc 4, inc)

Inner Ear Make 2

R1	With B, sc 6 in magic ring (6)
R2	[sc 3] in next st, inc, [sc 1, hdc 2] in next st, [hdc 2, sc 1] in next st, inc, [sc 3] in next st (16)
R3	sc 1, inc, sc 4, [sc 1, hdc 1] in next st, hdc 2, [hdc 1, sc 1] in next st, sc 4, inc, sc 1 (20)
R4	sc 9, [hdc 1, dc 1] in next st, [dc 1, hdc 1] in next st, sc 9 (22)

( ) Round brackets

The stitches within round brackets indicate a repeating pattern. For example, **(sc 1, inc) six times** means one sc in first stitch, one inc in next stitch, and repeat (sc 1, inc) five more times.

[ ] Square brackets

Square brackets contain the stitches that go into a single stitch. **[hdc 1, dc 1]** means crochet one hdc and one dc into the same stitch.

● Skill level

Skill levels range from one dot (easiest) to three dots (most challenging).

Bring an animal to life

For pictures and videos, visit crochetwildlifeguide.com.

Crochet hooks and yarn

The basic amigurumi supplies are a hook and yarn. Amigurumi stitches need to be tight to hold the shape and keep stuffing in, so use a crochet hook that is one to two hook sizes smaller than the yarn recommends. Hooks around 4 mm (G) to 5 mm (H) will create stitches that are tight enough to hold stuffing with medium worsted yarn.

Throughout an amigurumi project, keep the yarn tension tight. This also helps create rigid stitches.

Yarn comes in a variety of types and colors. Acrylic yarn is ideal for amigurumi because it holds shape, comes in many colors, can be easily washed and is hypoallergenic. Natural yarns tend to be softer, but they are more challenging to wash and create more droopy results.

Medium worsted weight yarn will produce a durable product with a tight gauge so the stuffing does not show through. As long as the stitches are tight, any weight of yarn would work. Use the same weight yarn for an entire project to keep all the pieces proportional.

Basic techniques

Slip Knot

This knot is used to start a chain.

With the yarn, form a circle and insert hook into circle (a). Pull top yarn end through (b). Tighten yarn around hook by pulling the tail end (c).

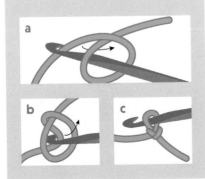

Chain stitch

Used to create a foundation chain.

From a slip knot, yarn over hook (a) and pull through loop on hook (b).

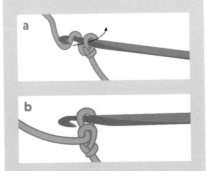

Slip stitch

This simple stitch is used to finish off the work or to connect pieces together.

Insert hook into stitch (a), yarn over hook and pull through stitch and loop on hook (b).

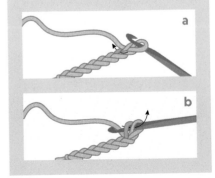

Stitches

Single crochet (double crochet in UK)

The most common stitch used in amigurumi.

At the beginning of a new row, insert hook into second stitch from hook (a). Yarn over and pull yarn through stitch (b). Yarn over and pull through both loops on hook (c). For next single crochet stitch, continue by inserting hook into next stitch (d).

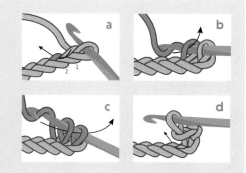

Half double crochet (half treble in UK)

This creates a stitch that is bigger than a single crochet, but works well to keep in stuffing.

At start of a new row, yarn over and insert hook into second stitch from hook (a). Yarn over and pull through stitch (b). Yarn over and pull through all three loops on hook (c). For next half double crochet stitch, yarn over and insert hook into next stitch.

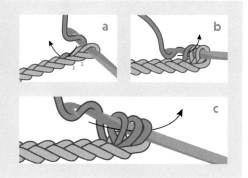

Double crochet (treble crochet in UK)

Twice the height of single crochet, double crochet is useful for flat embellishments and creating height. It does not hold in stuffing well.

At the beginning of a new row, yarn over and insert hook into third stitch (a). Yarn over and pull through stitch (b). Yarn over and pull through first two loops on hook (c). Yarn over and pull through final two loops on hook (d). For the next double crochet stitch, yarn over and insert hook into next stitch.

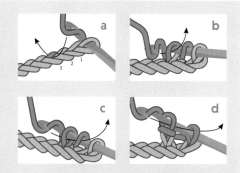

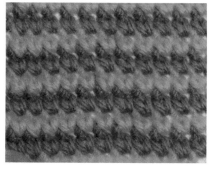

Single crochet

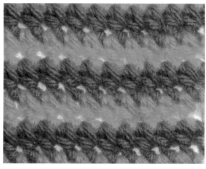

Half double crochet

Double crochet

Shaping

Increasing stitches

A crochet increase is a technique used to increase the width of a shape.

To create an increase, crochet two stitches into the same stitch (b).

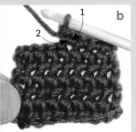

Decreasing stitches

A single crochet decrease is used to subtract stitches from a round or row.

Yarn over and insert hook into first stitch. Draw yarn through just the stitch (a). Yarn over and insert hook into second stitch (b). Yarn over and draw yarn through all loops on hook.

There are two major factors that impact the final shape of a 3D object: number of stitches in each round and the distribution of increases or decreases. The change in the number of stitches increased or decreased between rounds makes a shape either bigger or smaller. Equally distributing the increases or decreases creates shapes that are uniform, while clumping increases or decreases can form bulges.

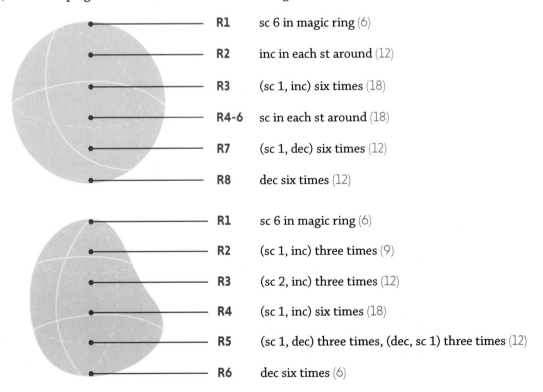

R1	sc 6 in magic ring (6)
R2	inc in each st around (12)
R3	(sc 1, inc) six times (18)
R4-6	sc in each st around (18)
R7	(sc 1, dec) six times (12)
R8	dec six times (12)

R1	sc 6 in magic ring (6)
R2	(sc 1, inc) three times (9)
R3	(sc 2, inc) three times (12)
R4	(sc 1, inc) six times (18)
R5	(sc 1, dec) three times, (dec, sc 1) three times (12)
R6	dec six times (6)

Starting rounds and rows

Magic ring start

The magic ring is used when crocheting in rounds. It forms a circle of stitches that can be tightened, leaving no hole in the center of the piece.

Wrap yarn around two fingers to create an X (a). Flip hand and pull back yarn under front yarn (b) and twist the loop (c). Yarn over (d) and pull through the loop on the hook. Remove the ring from fingers (e) and crochet required number of stitches into the center of the ring and around the tail (f). Pull tail to tighten the ring.

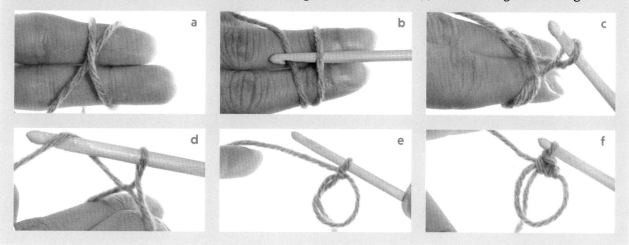

Foundation chain start

The foundation chain start is used when working in rows or non-circular rounds.

Chain required number of stitches (a). Skip the first chain from the hook and crochet as specified in pattern (b). If working in rows, chain 1 at the end of the row and turn piece around (d).

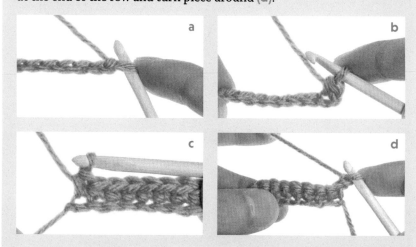

Keeping track of rounds

Crochet the first stitch in a round over a scrap piece of yarn (a) to keep track of where the round started and the number of stitches completed.

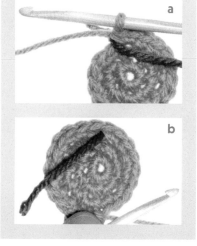

Special stitches and techniques

Changing yarn colors

Changing the yarn color from color A to color B can be done at the beginning or middle of a round or row.

The color change is done before finishing the previous stitch. Work the last stitch in color A until there are two loops remaining on the hook (a). Yarn over with color B (b) and draw through the two loops on the hook (c). Continue crocheting with color B (d). The tails of color A and color B are woven into the work with a yarn needle.

Puff stitch

The puff stitch is made by crocheting several unfinished double crochet stitches together into the same stitch. It forms a puff that is perfect for toes or fingers.

Yarn over (a), insert hook into stitch, yarn over, draw yarn through stitch (b). Yarn over, draw yarn through 2 loops on hook (c). Repeat two more times in the same stitch, ending with 4 loops on the hook (d). Yarn over and draw yarn through all 4 loops.

Latch hook stitch

Used to attach yarn strands to make hair or fur. The strands can be brushed out with a pet brush to make fluffy fur.

Draw a loop of yarn through an exterior stitch (c). Yarn over (d) and pull entire strand through loop (f).

Odds and ends

Stuffing

Before sewing together pieces, stuff animals until firm with polyester stuffing. Yarn scraps can work well too.

Joining and sewing together

To finish a piece, crochet a slip stitch, cut the yarn and pull the end through the stitch. The yarn tail can then be used to sew pieces together or weaved in to make it hidden.

Sew pieces together tightly and stuff the remaining yarn into the creature. No need for a final knot, just in case a piece needs to be moved.

Embroidery

To create secure and defined yarn embellishments, embroider twice with one piece of yarn. Stuff the ends in.

Felt

Felt resembles fine fur and can complement yarn. Use felt glue to attach the felt.

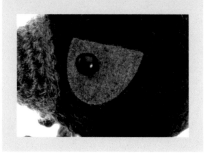

Safety eyes

Safety eyes have a clasp that ensures they cannot be pulled out. In all pictures, the size of the safety eyes used is 8 mm.

Crochet abbreviations

ch: chain
st: stitch
sc: single crochet
hdc: half double crochet
dc: double crochet
inc: increase
dec: decrease

sl st: slip stitch
yo: yarn over
RS: right side
WS: wrong side
rep: repeat
rnd: round

Rabbit
Oryctolagus cuniculus

Yarn Colors
Brown (A)
Beige (B)
Pink (C)

Notions
2 safety eyes
Stuffing

Measurements

13 cm

4 cm

8 cm

Skill Level ●○○

To better view predators and danger, rabbits can stand up on their hind legs.

Head

R1	With A, sc 6 into magic ring (6)
R2	inc in each st around (12)
R3	(sc 1, inc) six times (18)
R4	(sc 2, inc) six times (24)
R5	(sc 3, inc) six times (30)
R6	(sc 4, inc) six times (36)
R7-11	sc in each st around (36)
R12	sc 8, inc, inc, sc 16, inc, inc, sc 8 (40)
R13	sc 18, inc, sc 2, inc, sc 18 (42)
R14	sc in each st around (42)
R15	(sc 5, dec) three times, (dec, sc 5) three times (36)
R16	(sc 4, dec) six times (30)
R17	(sc 3, dec) six times (24)
R18	dec twelve times (12)

Finish with a sl st. Leave long tail for sewing.

Insert safety eyes and embroider nose with C.

Ears Make 2

R1	With A, sc 6 into magic ring (6)
R2	inc in each st around (12)
R3	(sc 3, inc) three times (15)
R4	(sc 4, inc) three times (18)
R5-7	sc in each st around (18)
R8	(sc 7, dec) two times (16)
R9	sc in each st around (16)
R10	(sc 6, dec) two times (14)
R11	sc in each st around (14)
R12	(sc 5, dec) two times (12)
R13	sc in each st around (12)
R14	(sc 4, dec) two times (10)
R15	sc in each st around (10)

Finish with a sl st. Leave long tail for sewing.

Embroider the nose one row below the eyes.

Switching yarns A and B to white can create a rabbit ready for the winter.

Feet Make 2

With A, ch 6.

R1	Skip first ch from hook, sc 4, inc, turn to work other side of the foundation chain, inc, sc 4 (12)
R2	sc 4, inc, inc, inc, inc, sc 4 (16)
R3	sc 5, (puff st, sc 1) three times, sc 5 (16)
R4	sc 4, dec four times, sc 4 (12)
R5	sc 3, dec, dec, dec, sc 3 (9)

Finish with a sl st. Leave short tail and weave in.

The body is created by joining together the feet and then working up. Attach the feet together by crocheting through both feet at once. Single crochet 2 through both pieces to work towards the heels of the feet.

At the middle of the back of the feet, begin crocheting in a round. Working all the way around the feet will directly connect the body to the two feet.

Body

With A, join the two feet by pulling a yarn loop through the stitches near the innermost toes. Crocheting into both pieces, sc 2.

The body will be crocheted in the round starting from the middle of the back.

R1	inc, sc 6, inc, inc, sc 6, inc (20)
R2-4	sc in each st around (20)
R5	(sc 8, dec) two times (18)
R6-7	sc in each st around (18)
R8	(sc 7, dec) two times (16)
R9	sc in each st around (16)
R10	(sc 2, dec) four times (12)
R11	sc in each st around (12)

Finish with a sl st. Leave short tail and weave in.

Arms Make 2

R1	With A, sc 6 into magic ring (6)
R2	inc in each st around (12)
R3	(sc 4, dec) two times (10)
R4	sc in each st around (10)
R5	(sc 3, dec) two times (8)
R6	sc in each st around (8)
R7	(sc 2, dec) two times (6)

Finish with a sl st. Leave long tail for sewing.

Tail

R1	With B, sc 6 into magic ring (6)
R2	inc in each st around (12)
R3	sc in each st around (12)
R4	(sc 4, dec) two times (10)
R5	(sc 3, dec) two times (8)

Finish with a sl st. Leave long tail for sewing.

The ears start with a magic ring at the tip and are worked in rounds. Flattening the ears make them sturdy and slightly indented.

To make assembly easier, attach the head to the body first. Then line up the top of the arms with the top row of the body to form shoulders.

Feet are made by starting at the sole and working up. Three puff stitches on the feet create three toes. Then the body is crocheted directly onto the feet.

Mountain Bluebird
Sialia currucoides

Yarn Colors
Light blue (A)
White (B)
Grey (C)

Notions
2 safety eyes
Stuffing

Measurements

10 cm
6 cm
8 cm

Skill Level ●○○

Head

R1	With A, sc 6 into magic ring (6)
R2	inc in each st around (12)
R3	(sc 1, inc) six times (18)
R4	(sc 2, inc) six times (24)
R5	(sc 3, inc) six times (30)
R6-8	sc in each st around (30)
R9	sc 7, inc, inc, sc 12, inc, inc, sc 7 (34)
R10-11	sc in each st around (34)
R12	(sc 15, dec) two times (32)
R13	(sc 14, dec) two times (30)
R14	(sc 3, dec) six times (24)
R15	(sc 2, dec) six times (18)
R16	(sc 1, dec) six times (12)

Finish with a sl st. Leave long tail for sewing.

Insert safety eyes.

Beak

R1	With C, sc 6 into magic ring (6)
R2	inc, inc, sc 2, inc, inc (10)
R3	sc in each st around (10)
R4	sc 1, inc, sc 6, inc, sc 1 (12)

Finish with a sl st. Leave long tail for sewing.

Body

R1	With B, sc 6 into magic ring (6)
R2	inc in each st around (12)
R3	(sc 1, inc) six times (18)
R4	(sc 2, inc) six times (24)

Make the belly white by switching between A and B in the rows.

R5	sc 4, switch to A, sc 7, inc, inc, sc 7, switch to B, sc 4 (26)
R6	sc 3, switch to A, sc 8, inc, sc 2, inc, sc 8, switch to B, sc 3 (28)
R7	sc 2, switch to A, sc 10, dec, dec, sc 12 (26)
R8	sc 11, dec, dec, sc 11 (24)
R9	(sc 2, dec) three times, (dec, sc 2) three times (18)
R10	(sc 1, dec) three times, (dec, sc 1) three times (12)

Finish with a sl st. Leave short tail and weave in.

Insert safety eyes and attach beak.

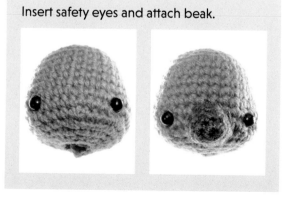

Robins have an orange belly and a grey head and body.

Feet Make 2

The feet are made in one continuous row. With C, chain 3.

1   Skip first ch from hook, sl st 2, ch 3
2   Skip first ch from hook, sl st 2, ch 4
3   Skip first ch from hook, sl st 3, ch 3
4   Skip first ch from hook, sl st 2

Finish with a sl st into initial chain.

Leave long tail for sewing.

The feet are made in just one row using chain stitches and slip stitches. Begin by chaining three, skipping first chain from hook, slip stitching twice then chaining three more stitches.

Continue creating the toes using a series of slip stitches and chain stitches. After the three front toes and one back toe have been created, connect them with a slip stitch into the original chain.

Wings Make 2

The wings are worked in rows. With A, chain 7.

R1   Skip first ch from hook, sc 6, ch 1 and turn
R2   Skip first ch from hook, sc 5, ch 3 and turn
R3   Skip first ch from hook, hdc 2, sc 5, ch 1 and turn
R4   Skip first ch from hook, sc 6, ch 1 and turn
R5   Skip first ch from hook, hdc 1, sc 5

Along edge of wing, sc 2. Finish with a sl st into last space on the edge.

Leave long tail for sewing.

To finish the wing, single crochet into two stitches along the front edge of the wing (b). Then finish with a slip stitch (c). This creates a slightly rounded finish on the front part of the wing (d).

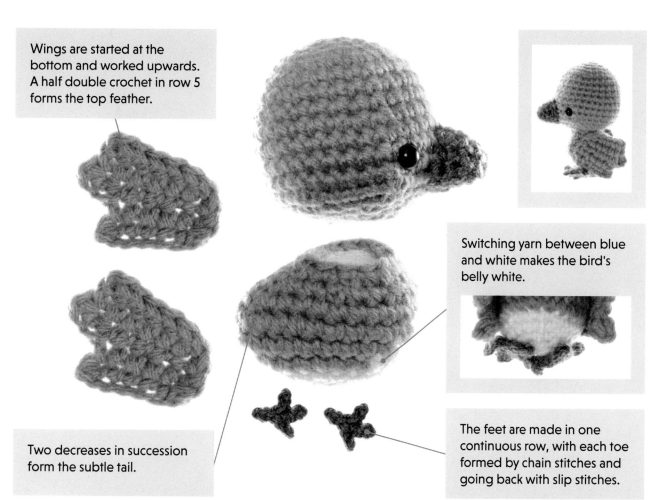

Wings are started at the bottom and worked upwards. A half double crochet in row 5 forms the top feather.

Switching yarn between blue and white makes the bird's belly white.

Two decreases in succession form the subtle tail.

The feet are made in one continuous row, with each toe formed by chain stitches and going back with slip stitches.

Flying Squirrel

Glaucomys volans

Yarn Colors
Light brown (A)
Cream (B)
Dark Brown (C)

Notions
2 safety eyes
Stuffing

Measurements

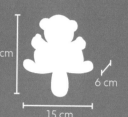

18 cm

6 cm

15 cm

Skill Level ● ● ●

Head

R1	With A, sc 6 into magic ring (6)
R2	inc in each st around (12)
R3	(sc 1, inc) six times (18)
R4	(sc 2, inc) six times (24)
R5	(sc 3, inc) six times (30)
R6-8	sc in each st around (30)
R9	sc 13, inc four times, sc 13 (34)
R10	sc 12, switch to B, sc 10, switch to A, sc 12 (34)
R11	Switch to B, sc 13, dec four times, sc 13 (30)
R12	sc in each st around (30)
R13	(sc 3, dec) six times (24)
R14	(sc 2, dec) six times (18)
R15	(sc 1, dec) six times (12)
R16	dec six times (6)

Finish with a sl st. Leave short tail and weave in.

Insert safety eyes and embroider nose with C.

Inner Ears Make 2

R1	With B, sc 3, hdc 1, sc 3 into magic ring (7)

Finish with a sl st. Leave short tail and weave in.

Outer Ears Make 2

R1	With A, sc 3, hdc 1, sc 3 into magic ring (7)

Lay inner ear piece over the outer ear with WS facing each other. Crochet the following row into both pieces.

R2	inc, sc 2, hdc 1, sc 2, inc (9)

Finish with a sl st. Leave long tail for sewing.

Body

R1	With A, sc 6 into magic ring (6)
R2	inc in each st around (12)
R3	(sc 1, inc) six times (18)
R4	(sc 2, inc) six times (24)
R5-8	sc in each st around (24)
R9	sc 9, dec, sc 2, dec, sc 9 (22)
R10	sc 8, dec, sc 2, dec, sc 8 (20)
R11	sc in each st around (20)
R12	(sc 8, dec) two times (18)
R13	(sc 7, dec) two times (16)
R14	(sc 6, dec) two times (14)

Finish with a sl st. Leave long tail for sewing.

Arms Make 2

R1	With A, 6 sc into magic ring (6)
R2	sc 1, inc four times, sc 1 (10)
R3	sc 2, (puff st, sc 1) three times, sc 2 (10)
R4	sc in each st around (10)
R5	(sc 3, dec) two times (8)
R6-8	sc in each st around (8)

Finish with a sl st. Leave long tail for sewing.

Flying squirrels use their flat tails as a rudder to direct themselves while gliding.

Feet Make 2

R1	With A, sc 6 in magic ring (6)
R2	inc, inc, sc 2, inc, inc (10)
R3	sc 4, inc, inc, sc 4 (12)
R4	sc in each st around (12)
R5	sc 4, dec, dec, sc 4 (10)
R6	sc 3, dec, dec, sc 3 (8)
R7	sc 2, dec, dec, sc 2 (6)
R8	sc 1, inc four times, sc 1 (10)
R9	sc in each st around (10)
R10	sc 4, inc, inc, sc 4 (12)
R11	sc in each st around (12)
R12	(sc 3, inc) three times (15)
R13	sc in each st around (15)

Finish with a sl st. Leave long tail for sewing.

Wings Make 2

The wings are worked in rows.

With A, chain 4.

R1	Skip first ch from hook, sc 3, ch 1 and turn
R2	Skip first ch from hook, inc, sc 2, ch 1 and turn
R3	Skip first ch from hook, sc 2, inc, inc, ch 1 and turn
R4	Skip first ch from hook, sc 1, inc, sc 4, ch 1 and turn
R5	Skip first ch from hook, sc 5, inc, sc 1

Fasten off. Leave long tail for sewing.

The tail is made of two identical pieces, one brown and one beige. They are attached with a row of brown.

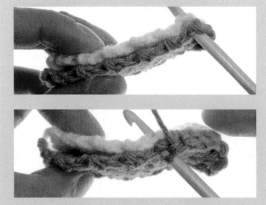

Belly

The belly is worked in rows. With B, chain 4.

R1	Skip first ch from hook, sc 3, ch 1 and turn
R2	Skip first ch from hook, sc 1, inc, sc 1, ch 1 and turn
R3	Skip first ch from hook, sc 1, inc, sc 2, ch 1 and turn
R4	Skip first ch from hook, sc 2, inc, sc 2, ch 1 and turn
R5-7	Skip first ch from hook, sc 6, ch 1 and turn
R8	Skip first ch from hook, dec, sc 2, dec, ch 1 and turn
R9	Skip first ch from hook, sc 4, ch 1 and turn
R10	Skip first ch from hook, sc 1, dec, sc 1

Working around the edge of the belly, sc 21. Finish with a sl st. Leave long tail for sewing.

Tail

The tail is worked in rows. Make one piece in A (top of tail) and make one piece in B (tail underside). With A/B, chain 4.

R1-2	Skip first ch from hook, sc 3, ch 1 and turn
R3	Skip first ch from hook, sc 1, inc, sc 1, ch 1 and turn
R4	Skip first ch from hook, sc 1, inc, inc, sc 1, ch 1 and turn
R5-9	Skip first ch from hook, sc 6, ch 1 and turn
R10	Skip first ch from hook, sc 2, dec, sc 2, ch 1 and turn
R11	Skip first ch from hook, sc 5, ch 1 and turn
R12	Skip first ch from hook, dec, sc 1, dec

Fasten off. Leave short tail and weave in.

Lay both pieces over one another and crochet the following row through both pieces. With A, pull a yarn loop through the bottom tip of tail.

Working around the edge of the tail, sc 25. Finish with a sl st. Leave long tail for sewing.

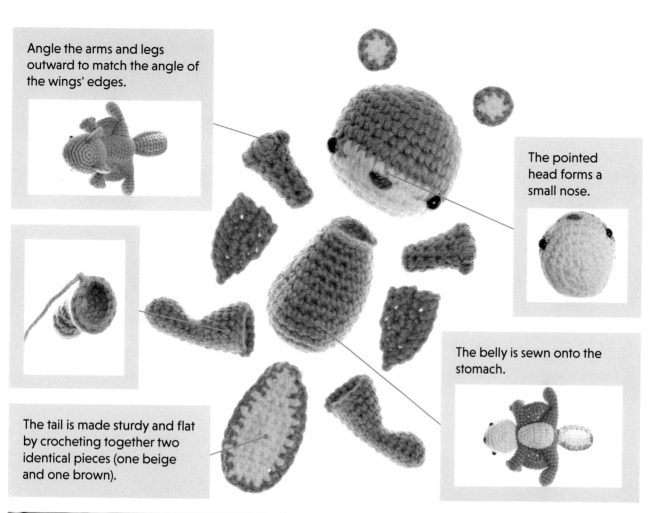

Angle the arms and legs outward to match the angle of the wings' edges.

The pointed head forms a small nose.

The tail is made sturdy and flat by crocheting together two identical pieces (one beige and one brown).

The belly is sewn onto the stomach.

River Otter

Lontra canadensis

Yarn Colors
Brown (A)
Cream (B)
Black (C)
Pink (D)

Notions
2 safety eyes
Stuffing
White felt

Measurements

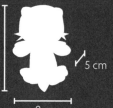

13 cm

5 cm

8 cm

Skill Level ●○○

Head

R1 With A, sc 6 into magic ring (6)
R2 inc in each st around (12)
R3 (sc 1, inc) six times (18)
R4 (sc 2, inc) six times (24)
R5 (sc 3, inc) six times (30)
R6-9 sc in each st around (30)
R10 sc 6, inc, inc, switch to B, sc 6, switch to A, sc 2, switch to B, sc 6, switch to A, inc, inc, sc 6 (34)
R11 sc 10, switch to B, sc 14, switch to A, sc 10 (34)
R12 sc 10, switch to B, sc 5, inc, sc 2, inc, sc 5, switch to A, sc 10 (36)
R13 sc 4, dec, sc 4, switch to B, dec, (sc 4, dec) two times, sc 2, switch to A, sc 2, dec, sc 4, dec (30)
R14 (sc 3, dec) two times, switch to B, (sc 3, dec) two times, sc 2, switch to A, sc, dec, sc 3, dec (24)
R15 dec four times, switch to B, dec four times, switch to A, dec four times (12)

Finish with a sl st. Leave long tail for sewing.

Insert safety eyes and embroider nose with C. See page 64 for the whisker felt template.

Embroider nose in the same row as the eyes, and glue whiskers two rows below.

Body

R1 With A, sc 6 into magic ring (6)
R2 inc in each st around (12)
R3 (sc 1, inc) six times (18)
R4 (sc 2, inc) six times (24)
R5-7 sc in each st around (24)
R8 (sc 4, dec) four times (20)
R9 (sc 8, dec) two times (18)
R10-11 sc in each st around (18)
R12 sc 7, switch to B, dec, sc 1, switch to A, sc 6, dec (16)
R13 sc 6, switch to B, sc 4, switch to A, sc 6 (16)
R14 sc 3, dec, switch to B, sc 6, switch to A, dec, sc 3 (14)
R15 sc 1, dec, sc 1, switch to B, sc 6, switch to A, sc 1, dec, sc 1 (12)

Finish with a sl st. Leave short tail and weave in.

From rows 12 to 15, switch briefly from brown to beige.

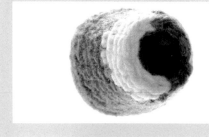

Ears Make 2

R1   With A, sc 6 into magic ring (6)
R2   (sc 1, inc) three times (9)

Finish with a sl st. Leave long tail for sewing.

Arms Make 2

R1   With A, sc 6 into magic ring (6)
R2   inc in each st around (12)
R3   (sc 4, dec) two times (10)
R4   sc 1, puff st, sc 8 (10)
R5   (sc 3, dec) two times (8)
R6   (sc 2, dec) two times (6)
R7   sc in each st around (6)

Finish with a sl st. Leave long tail for sewing.

One puff stitch in row 4 creates the thumb on the arms. After crocheting a puff stitch **(a)**, continue with single crochets in the following stitches **(b)**. The thumb's orientation on the arm can be adjusted by changing the location of the puff stitch within row 4.

Feet Make 2

R1   With A, sc 6 into magic ring (6)
R2   sc 1, inc four times, sc 1 (10)
R3   sc 2, (puff st, sc 1) three times, sc 2 (10)
R4   (sc 3, dec) two times (8)

Finish with a sl st. Leave long tail for sewing.

Tail

R1   With A, sc 5 into magic ring (5)
R2   sc 2, inc, sc 2 (6)
R3   (sc 2, inc) two times (8)
R4   sc 3, inc, sc 4 (9)
R5-6   sc in each st around (9)

Finish with a sl st. Leave long tail for sewing.

Scallop

The scallop is worked in rows. With D, chain 4.

R1   Skip first ch from hook, hdc 1, sc 1, sl st 1, ch 1 and turn
R2   Skip first ch from hook, sl st 1, sc 2, ch 1 and turn
R3   Skip first ch from hook, hdc 1, sc 1, sl st 1, ch 1 and turn
R4   Skip first ch from hook, sl st 1, sc 2, ch 1 and turn
R5   Skip first ch from hook, hdc 1, sc 1, sl st 1

Fasten off. Leave long tail for sewing.

Repeat **R1-5** to make a second shell. Sew the two shells together to form a complete scallop.

The scallop is made with two identical shells. They are crocheted in rows, starting at one side and working across. After sewing the shells together, the yarn ends can be stuffed inside the scallop to make it slightly puffy.

Attach feet and tail to base of body, two rows from the magic loop.

Switch between beige and brown in the head and body.

See page 64 for felt template.

One puff stitch creates the thumbs in the arms. Three puff stitches form the toes on the feet.

Grey Bat

Myotis grisescens

Yarn Colors
Grey (A)
Brown (B)

Notions
2 safety eyes
Stuffing
White felt

Measurements
14 cm
6 cm
14 cm

Skill Level ●●○

Head and Body

R1	With A, sc 6 into magic ring (6)
R2	inc in each st around (12)
R3	(sc 1, inc) six times (18)
R4	(sc 2, inc) six times (24)
R5	(sc 3, inc) six times (30)
R6	(sc 4, inc) six times (36)
R7-10	sc in each st around (36)
R11	sc 8, inc, inc, sc 16, inc, inc, sc 8 (40)
R12	sc in each st around (40)
R13	sc 18, inc, sc 2, inc, sc 18 (42)
R14	sc in each st around (42)
R15	(sc 5, dec) six times (36)
R16	(sc 4, dec) six times (30)
R17	(sc 3, dec) six times (24)

Cut felt (template on page 64). Insert safety eyes through felt and onto head. Glue felt onto head.

R18	dec twelve times (12)
R19	(sc 1, inc) six times (18)
R20	(sc 2, inc) six times (24)
R21	sc in each st around (24)
R22	(sc 4, dec) four times (20)
R23	sc in each st around (20)
R24	(sc 3, dec) four times (16)
R25	sc in each st around (16)
R26	(sc 2, dec) four times (12)
R27	dec six times (6)

Finish with a sl st. Leave short tail and weave in.

Inner Ears Make 2

R1	With B, sc 6 into magic ring (6)
R2	[sc 3] in next st, inc, hdc 2, inc, [sc 3] in next st (12)
R3	sc 1, inc, sc 3, [sc 1, hdc] in next st, [hdc, sc 1] in next st, sc 3, inc, sc 1 (16)

Finish with a sl st. Leave short tail and weave in.

Outer Ears Make 2

R1	With A, sc 6 into magic ring (6)
R2	[sc 3] in next st, inc, hdc 2, inc, [sc 3] in next st (12)
R3	sc 1, inc, sc 3, [sc 1, hdc] in next st, [hdc, sc 1] in next st, sc 3, inc, sc 1 (16)

Lay inner ear piece over the outer ear with WS facing each other. In the following row, crochet into both pieces.

R4	sc 1, inc, inc, sc 4, [sc 1, hdc 1] in next st, [hdc 1, sc 1] in next st, sc 4, inc, inc, sc 1 (22)

Finish with a sl st. Leave long tail for sewing.

The outer ear and inner ear are the same shape. They are then attached by crocheting into both pieces all the way around.

Wings Make 2

The wings are worked in rows. With B, ch 6.

R1 Skip first ch from hook, sc 5, ch 1 and turn

R2 Skip first ch from hook, dec, sc 2, inc, ch 1 and turn

R3 Skip first ch from hook, sc 5, ch 1 and turn

R4 Skip first ch from hook, inc, sc 4, ch 1 and turn

R5 Skip first ch from hook, sc 5, inc, ch 1 and turn

R6 Skip first ch from hook, sc 5, dec, ch 1 and turn

R7 Skip first ch from hook, sc 4, dec, ch 1 and turn

R8 Skip first ch from hook, dec, sc 1, dec, ch 1 and turn

R9 Skip first ch from hook, sc 3

Fasten off. Leave long tail for sewing.

Crochet the wing membrane using a surface slip stitch. Hold wing with right side facing and yarn at the back. With A, insert hook into the top of the wing and draw up a loop. Slip stitch into the wing one stitch lower. Repeat five more times. Finish with one sl st. Cut short tail and weave in.

With the right side facing and yarn at the back, insert hook into the tip of the wing and draw up a loop. Along the top edge of the wing, sc 9, inc, sc 3.

Fasten off. Leave long tail for sewing.

Feet Make 2

R1 With A, sc 6 in magic ring (6)

R2 sc 2, inc, inc, sc 2 (8)

R3 sc 3, inc, inc, sc 3 (10)

R4 sc 3, puff st, sl st, sl st, puff st, sc 3 (10)

R5 sc 3, dec, dec, sc 3 (8)

Finish with a sl st. Leave long tail for sewing.

Tail

R1 With A, sc 5 in magic ring (5)

R2 sc 2, inc, sc 2 (6)

R3 (sc 1, inc) three times (9)

Finish with a sl st. Leave long tail for sewing.

The two feet are attached at the bottom of the body, and the little tail sticks out the back.

Surface slip stitches form the wing membrane. Insert the hook in a stitch (a) and pull a loop through (b). Insert the hook into the wing one stitch below and draw a second loop (c) and pull through the first loop. Continue working down the wing (d). Add the top edge (e).

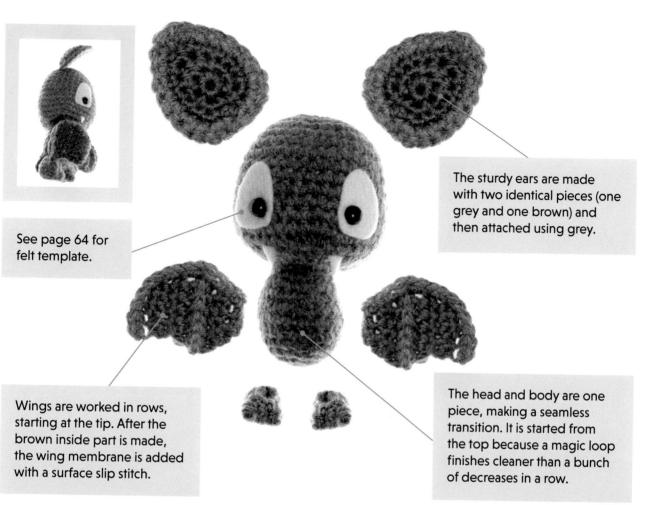

See page 64 for felt template.

The sturdy ears are made with two identical pieces (one grey and one brown) and then attached using grey.

Wings are worked in rows, starting at the tip. After the brown inside part is made, the wing membrane is added with a surface slip stitch.

The head and body are one piece, making a seamless transition. It is started from the top because a magic loop finishes cleaner than a bunch of decreases in a row.

Brown Bear

Ursus arctos

Yarn Colors
Brown (A)
Beige (B)
Dark Brown (C)

Notions
2 safety eyes
Stuffing

Measurements

13 cm
9 cm
10 cm

Skill Level ●○○

Head

R1	With A, sc 6 into magic ring (6)
R2	inc in each st around (12)
R3	(sc 1, inc) six times (18)
R4	(sc 2, inc) six times (24)
R5	(sc 3, inc) six times (30)
R6	(sc 4, inc) six times (36)
R7-11	sc in each st around (36)
R12	sc 8, inc, inc, sc 16, inc, inc, sc 8 (40)
R13-15	sc in each st around (40)
R16	(sc 8, dec) four times (36)
R17	(sc 4, dec) six times (30)
R18	(sc 3, dec) six times (24)
R19	dec twelve times (12)

Finish with a sl st. Leave long tail for sewing.

Insert safety eyes.

Muzzle

R1	With B, sc 6 into magic ring (6)
R2	inc, inc, sc 2, inc, inc (10)
R3	(sc 1, inc) two times, sc 2, (inc, sc 1) two times (14)
R4	sc 2, inc, sc 8, inc, sc 2 (16)

Finish with a sl st. Leave long tail for sewing. Embroider the nose with C.

Ears Make 2

R1	With A, sc 6 into magic ring (6)
R2	inc in st around (12)
R3	(sc 3, inc) three times (15)
R4	sc in each st around (15)

Finish with a sl st. Leave long tail for sewing.

Brown bear cubs can climb trees but they lose this ability after they gain weight.

The bear's cheeks are formed by placing two increases in succession in row 12.

Body

R1	With A, sc 6 into magic ring (6)
R2	inc in each st around (12)
R3	(sc 1, inc) six times (18)
R4	(sc 2, inc) six times (24)
R5	(sc 3, inc) six times (30)
R6-8	sc in each st around (30)
R9	(sc 3, dec) three times, (dec, sc 3) three times (24)
R10	sc in each st around (24)
R11	(sc 4, dec) four times (20)
R12	sc in each st around (20)
R13	(sc 3, dec) four times (16)
R14-15	sc in each st around (16)

Finish with a sl st. Leave short tail and weave in.

Tail

R1	With A, sc 6 into magic ring (6)
R2	inc in st around (12)
R3-4	sc in each st around (12)
R5	(sc 1, dec) four times (8)

Finish with a sl st. Leave long tail for sewing.

The rapid decreases in the final row bring the tail together. Finish by pinching the ends and sewing the tail together.

Feet Make 2

R1	With A, sc 7 in magic ring (7)
R2	inc in each st around (14)
R3	sc 4, (puff st, sc 1) three times, sc 4 (14)
R4-5	sc in each st around (14)
R6	(sc 5, dec) two times (12)

Finish with a sl st. Leave long tail for sewing.

Arms Make 2

R1	With A, sc 6 into magic ring (6)
R2	inc in each st around (12)
R3-4	sc in each st around (12)
R5	puff st, sc 11 (12)
R6	(sc 4, dec) around (10)
R7	sc in each st around (10)
R8	(sc 3, dec) around (8)
R9-10	sc in each st around (8)
R11	(sc 2, dec) around (6)

Finish with a sl st. Leave long tail for sewing.

The ears are half spheres that are flattened, and they are small enough that they don't have to be stuffed.

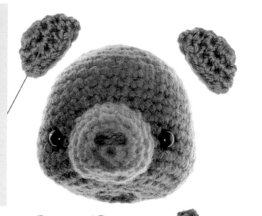

Having two decreases in succession in row 8 forms the bear's belly.

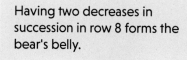

Great Horned Owl
Bubo virginianus

Yarn Colors
Brown (A)
Dark brown (B)
Beige (C)
Yellow (D)
Gray (E)
Black (F)

Notions
2 safety eyes
Stuffing

Measurements
14 cm
8 cm
7 cm

Skill Level ● ● ○

Eyes Make 2

The eye starts with a magic ring but is worked in rows.

R1	With D, sc 4 in magic ring, ch 1 and turn (4)
R2	Skip first ch from hook, inc in each st, switch to F, ch 1 and turn (8)
R3	Skip first ch from hook, (sc 1, inc) four times, switch to C, ch 1 and turn (12)
R4	Skip first ch from hook, (sc 2, inc) four times (16)

Fasten off. Leave long tail for sewing.

Head

R1	With A, sc 6 into magic ring (6)
R2	inc in each st around (12)
R3	(sc 1, inc) six times (18)
R4	(sc 2, inc) six times (24)
R5	(sc 3, inc) six times (30)
R6	(sc 4, inc) six times (36)
R7-11	sc in each st around (36)
R12	sc 10, inc, inc, sc 12, inc, inc, sc 10 (40)
R13-14	sc in each st around (40)
R15	(sc 8, dec) four times (36)
R16	sc in each st around (36)
R17	(sc 4, dec) six times (30)
R18	(sc 3, dec) six times (24)
R19	dec twelve times (12)

Finish with a sl st. Leave long tail for sewing.

Insert safety eyes through eyes and head. Sew eyes onto head at an angle.

Brow

The brow is worked in rows. Make two identical pieces, a left side and right side. With B, ch 3.

R1	Skip first ch from hook, sc 2, ch 1 and turn
R2	Skip first ch from hook, inc, sc 1, ch 1 and turn
R3	Skip first ch from hook, sc 2, inc, ch 1 and turn
R4-6	Skip first ch from hook, sc 4, ch 1 and turn
R7	Skip first ch from hook, [hdc 2] in next st, sc 3, ch 1 and turn
R8	Skip first ch from hook, sc 3, hdc 2, ch 1 and turn
R9	Skip first ch from hook, hdc 2, sc 1, dec, ch 1 and turn
R10	Skip first ch from hook, sc 2, hdc 2

Fasten off. Leave long tail for sewing.

Sew both sides of the brow together. Crochet along the top edge, starting from the tip of the brow. With C, sc 10, dec, dec, sc 10.

Fasten off. Leave short tail and weave in.

Beak

R1	With E, sc 5 into magic ring (5)
R2	sc 2, inc, sc 2 (6)
R3	inc, inc, sc 2, inc, inc (10)
R4	(sc 1, inc) five times (15)

Finish with a sl st. Leave long tail for sewing

Body

R1	With A, sc 6 into magic ring (6)
R2	inc in each st around (12)
R3	(sc 1, inc) six times (18)
R4	(sc 2, inc) six times (24)
R5	(sc 3, inc) three times, (inc, sc 3) three times (30)
R6	sc in each st around (30)
R7	sc 13, dec, dec, sc 13 (28)
R8	sc in each st around (28)
R9	(sc 5, dec) four times (24)
R10	sc in each st around (24)
R11	(sc 4, dec) four times (20)
R12	sc in each st around (20)
R13	(sc 3, dec) four times (16)
R14	sc in each st around (16)

Finish with a sl st. Leave short tail and weave in.

The two decreases in succession in row 7 curve the tip of the beak downwards.

Wings Make 2

Wings are worked in rows.

With B, ch 9.

R1	Skip first ch from hook, sc 8, ch 1 and turn
R2	Skip first ch from hook, sc 7, ch 3 and turn
R3	Skip first two ch from hook, hdc 2, sc 6, ch 1 and turn
R4	Skip first ch from hook, sc 8, ch 3 and turn
R5	Skip first two ch from hook, hdc 2, sc 1, [sc 1, ch 1, hdc] in next st, sc 5

Along the edge, sc 6, ch 1, [hdc 1, sl st] in next st

Fasten off. Leave long tail for sewing.

Feet Make 2

The feet are made in one continuous row.

With E, chain 4.

1	Skip first ch from hook, sc 3, ch 4
2	Skip first ch from hook, sc 3, ch 4
3	Skip first ch from hook, sc 3, ch 4
4	Skip first ch from hook, sc 3

Finish with a sl st into initial chain.

Brows are attached together before fixed to the head.

Half circles are created by starting with a magic ring and then working in rows.

The little feathers are made by crocheting along the edge, using half double and slip stitches to create the tips.

Back-to-back decreases form the pointed tail on the body.

Raven

Corvus corax

Yarn Colors
Black (A)
Grey (B)

Notions
2 safety eyes
Stuffing
Grey felt

Measurements

11 cm

7 cm

12 cm

Skill Level ●●○

Head

R1	With A, sc 6 into magic ring (6)
R2	inc in each st around (12)
R3	(sc 1, inc) six times (18)
R4	(sc 2, inc) six times (24)
R5	(sc 3, inc) six times (30)
R6	(sc 4, inc) six times (36)
R7-10	sc in each st around (36)
R11	sc 8, inc, inc, sc 16, inc, inc, sc 8 (40)
R12-14	sc in each st around (40)
R15	(sc 8, dec) four times (36)
R16	(sc 4, dec) six times (30)
R17	(sc 3, dec) six times (24)
R18	dec around (12)

Finish with a sl st. Leave long tail for sewing.

Cut felt using template on page 64. Insert safety eyes through felt and onto head, and glue felt onto head.

Body

R1	With A, sc 6 into magic ring (6)
R2	inc in each st around (12)
R3	(sc 1, inc) six times (18)
R4	(sc 2, inc) three times, (inc, sc 2) three times (24)
R5	(sc 3, inc) three times, (inc, sc 3) three times (30)
R6	sc in each st around (30)
R7	sc 14, inc, inc, sc 14 (32)
R8	sc 14, inc, sc 2, inc, sc 14 (34)
R9	sc in each st around (34)
R10	sc 13, dec four times, sc 13 (30)
R11	(sc 3, dec) three times, (dec, sc 3) three times (24)
R12	(sc 2, dec) three times, (dec, sc 2) three times (18)
R13	(sc 7, dec) two times (16)

Finish with a sl st. Leave a short tail and weave in.

Beak

R1	With B, sc 6 into magic ring (6)
R2	(sc 1, inc) three times (9)
R3	sc 3, inc, sc 5 (10)
R4	sc 4, inc, inc, sc 4 (12)
R5	inc, sc 10, inc (14)
R6	sc 1, inc, sc 10, inc, sc 1 (16)
R7	sc 2, inc, sc 10, inc, sc 2 (18)
R8	sc 3, inc, sc 4, [sc 1, hdc 1] in next st, [hdc 1, sc 1] in next st, sc 4, inc, sc 3 (22)

Finish with a sl st. Leave long tail for sewing.

Ravens are highly intelligent. They can craft tools, mimic noises and hide food for later.

Wings Make 2

Flying Wings

The flying wings are worked in a continuous row. With A, chain 11.

1   Skip first 2 ch from hook, hdc 4, sc 5, ch 8 and turn
2   Skip first ch from hook, sc 4, hdc 3, sc 1 into foundation ch, ch 8 and turn
3   Skip first ch from hook, sc 4, hdc 3, sc 1 into foundation ch, ch 7 and turn
4   Skip first ch from hook, sc 6, sc 1 into foundation ch, ch 6 and turn
5   Skip first ch from hook, sc 5, sc 1 into foundation ch, ch 6 and turn
6   Skip first ch from hook, sc 5, sc 1 into foundation ch, ch 6 and turn
7   Skip first ch from hook, sc 5, sc 1 into foundation ch, ch 5 and turn
8   Skip first ch from hook, sc 4, sc 1 into foundation ch, ch 4 and turn
9   Skip first ch from hook, sc 3, sl st 1 into foundation ch

Fasten off. Leave long tail for sewing.

Roosting Wings

The roosting wings are worked in rows. With A, chain 9.

R1   Skip first ch from hook, hdc 1, sc 7, ch 1 and turn
R2   Skip first ch from hook, sc 7, ch 3 and turn
R3   Skip first ch from hook, hdc 3, sc 6, ch 1 and turn
R4   Skip first ch from hook, sc 7, ch 2 and turn
R5   Skip first ch from hook, hdc 2, sc 6

Along the edge of wing, dec, sc 5, hdc 1. Fasten off. Leave long tail for sewing.

Roosting wings are similar in design to the mountain blue bird's wings.

Flying wings are larger and more splayed. They are made in one continuous row, with feathers crocheted into the foundation chain. The step numbers correspond to the feathers on the wing.

Connect the feathers into the foundation chain with a single crochet before chains.

Feet Make 2

The feet are made in one continuous row. With B, chain 4.

1   Skip first ch from hook, sl st 3, ch 4
2   Skip first ch from hook, sl st 3, ch 4
3   Skip first ch from hook, sl st 3, ch 4
4   Skip first ch from hook, sl st 3

Finish with a sl st into initial chain.

Tail

The tail is worked in rows. With A, chain 5.

R1   Skip first ch from hook, sc 3, sl st 1, ch 1 and turn
R2   Skip first ch from hook, sc 3, ch 2 and turn
R3   Skip first ch from hook, hdc 1, sc 2, sl st 1, ch 1 and turn
R4   Skip first ch from hook, sc 3, ch 1 and turn
R5   Skip first ch from hook, sl st 3

Fasten off. Leave long tail for sewing.

Stitches are reduced on the bottom of the beak to curve it downward.

Wings are worked in rows, with half double stitches adding feather-like tips. The flying wings are made in one continuous row.

See page 64 for felt template.

The wing is made in rows, starting at one side and working across.

Feet are made with just one continuous row.

Three-Toed Sloth

Bradypus variegatus

Yarn Colors
Brown (A)
Dark brown (B)
Cream (C)
Black (D)

Notions
2 safety eyes
Stuffing

Measurements

12 cm
7 cm
16 cm

Skill Level ●●○

Head

R1	With A, sc 6 in magic ring (6)
R2	inc in each st around (12)
R3	(sc 1, inc) six times (18)
R4	(sc 2, inc) six times (24)
R5	(sc 3, inc) six times (30)
R6-8	sc in each st around (30)
R9	sc 6, inc, inc, sc 14, inc, inc, sc 6 (34)
R10-11	sc in each st around (34)
R12	sc 6, dec, sc 18, dec, sc 6 (32)
R13	(sc 2, dec) eight times (24)
R14	(sc 2, dec) six times (18)

Finish with a sl st. Leave long tail for sewing.

The sloth's face is made from four pieces: the head, the cream front face and two dark brown eye spots. Sew the face onto the head first. Safety eyes go through the eye spot, face and head.

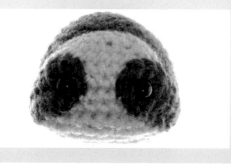

Face

The face is worked in rows. With C, chain 5.

R1	Skip first ch from hook, inc, sc 2, inc, ch 1 and turn
R2	Skip first ch from hook, inc, sc 4, inc, ch 1 and turn
R3	Skip first ch from hook, inc, sc 6, inc, ch 1 and turn
R4	Skip first ch from hook, sc 10, ch 1 and turn
R5	Skip first ch from hook, inc, inc, sc 6, inc, inc, ch 1 and turn
R6-7	Skip first ch from hook, sc 14, ch 1 and turn
R8	Skip first ch from hook, dec, dec, sc 6, dec, dec, ch 1 and turn
R9	Skip first ch from hook, dec, sc 6, dec, ch 1 and turn

Along the edge of the face, sc 28.

Finish with a sl st. Leave long tail for sewing.

Eye spots Make 2

With B, chain 8.

R1	Skip two ch from hook, [dc 2] in next st, hdc 1, sc 3, sl st 1, turn to work other side of foundation ch, sl st 1, sc 3, hdc 1, sc 1

Finish with a sl st. Leave long tail for sewing.

Nose

R1	With D, sc 6 in magic ring (6)
R2	inc, inc, sc 2, inc, inc (10)

Finish with a sl st. Leave long tail for sewing.

In addition to hanging in trees, three-toed sloths use their long arms to swim in rivers.

Body

R1	With A, sc 6 in magic ring	(6)
R2	inc in each st around	(12)
R3	(sc 1, inc) six times	(18)
R4	(sc 2, inc) six times	(24)
R5-6	sc in each st around	(24)
R7	(sc 4, dec) four times	(20)
R8	sc in each st around	(20)
R9	(sc 3, dec) four times	(16)
R10	(sc 6, dec) two times	(14)
R11	sc in each st around	(14)

Finish with a sl st. Leave a short tail and weave in.

Legs Make 2

R1	With A, sc 6 in magic ring	(6)
R2	inc in each st around	(12)
R3-5	sc in each st around	(12)
R6	(sc 4, dec) two times	(10)
R7	sc in each st around	(10)
R8	(sc 3, dec) two times	(8)

Finish with a sl st. Leave long tail for sewing.

Foot claws Make 3

R1	With B, sc 4 in magic ring	(4)
R2	sc 2, inc, sc 1	(5)

Finish with a sl st. Leave long tail for sewing.

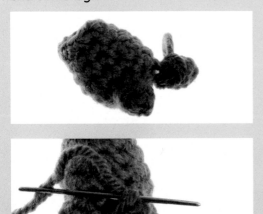

The foot claws are sewn onto the closed end of the leg.

Arms Make 2

When making the magic ring in **R1**, leave a long tail for sewing to body.

R1	With A, sc 6 in magic ring	(6)
R2	(sc 2, inc) two times	(8)
R3-4	sc in each st around	(8)
R5	(sc 3, inc) two times	(10)
R6-7	sc in each st around	(10)
R8	(sc 4, inc) two times	(12)
R9-10	sc in each st around	(12)
R11	(sc 3, inc) three times	(15)
R12	sc in each st around	(15)

Finish with a sl st. Leave long tail for sewing.

Hand claws Make 3

R1	With B, sc 4 in magic ring	(4)
R2	sc 2, inc, sc 1	(5)
R3	sc 2, inc, sc 2	(6)
R4-6	sc in each st around	(6)

Finish with a sl st. Leave short tail and weave in.

Join the hand claws to the arm opening, keeping the claws aligned with the arm. The magic ring end is sewn onto the body.

The face is a separate piece.

Eye spots are created in just one round by working on both sides of a foundation chain. They are sewn onto the face and head.

The hand claws are longer than the feet claws.

By equally spacing out the increases and decreases, the body is a uniform shape.

Axolotl

Ambystoma mexicanum

Yarn Colors
Light pink (A)
Dark pink (B)

Notions
2 safety eyes
Stuffing

Measurements

15 cm

5 cm

8 cm

Skill Level ●●○

Head

R1	With A, sc 8 in magic ring (8)
R2	sc 1, inc, inc, sc 2, inc, inc, sc 1 (12)
R3	sc 1, inc, inc, sc 6, inc, inc, sc 1 (16)
R4	(sc 3, inc) two times, (inc, sc 3) two times (20)
R5	(sc 4, inc) four times (24)
R6	(sc 3, inc) six times (30)
R7	sc in each st around (30)
R8	(sc 4, inc) six times (36)
R9-11	sc in each st around (36)
R12	sc 7, dec, dec, sc 14, dec, dec, sc 7 (32)
R13	(sc 6, dec) four times (28)
R14	(sc 2, dec) seven times (21)
R15	(sc 1, dec) seven times (14)
R16	dec 7 times (7)

Finish with a sl st. Leave short tail and weave in.

Insert safety eyes.

Body

R1	With A, sc 6 in magic ring (6)
R2	inc in each st around (12)
R3	(sc 1, inc) six times (18)
R4	(sc 2, inc) six times (24)
R5	(sc 3, inc) six times (30)
R6	sc in each st around (30)
R7	(sc 3, dec) three times, (dec, sc 3) three times (24)
R8	sc in each st around (24)
R9	(sc 4, dec) four times (20)
R10-11	sc in each st around (20)
R12	(sc 8, dec) two times (18)
R13	sc in each st around (18)
R14	(sc 7, dec) two times (16)

Finish with a sl st. Leave long tail for sewing.

Gill Frills Make 6

The frill is made in one continuous row.

With B, ch 8.

1	Skip first ch from hook, sc 1, sl st 1, ch 3
2	Skip first ch from hook, sl st 2, sl st 3 into foundation ch, ch 2
3	Skip first ch from hook, sl st 1, sl st 2 into foundation ch, ch 1
4	Turn to work other side of foundation ch, sl st 2, ch 2
5	Skip first ch from hook, sl st 1, sl st 3 into foundation ch, ch 3
6	Skip first ch from hook, sl st 2, sl st 1 into foundation ch, sc 1

Fasten off. Leave long tail for sewing.

Tail

R1 With A, sc 5 in magic ring (5)
R2 sc 2, inc, sc 2 (6)
R3 (sc 1, inc) three times (9)
R4 sc in each st around (9)
R5 (sc 2, inc) three times (12)
R6 sc in each st around (12)
R7 (sc 3, inc) three times (15)
R8 sc in each st around (15)
R9 (sc 4, inc) three times (18)
R10 sc in each st around (18)
R11 (sc 5, inc) three times (21)
R12 sc in each st around (21)

Finish with a sl st. Leave long tail for sewing.

Tail Fins

With B, ch 13.

R1 Skip first ch from hook, sc 5, hdc 3, sc 3, sl st 1

Fasten off. Leave long tail for sewing.

With B, ch 10.

R1 Skip first ch from hook, sc 4, hdc 2, sc 2, sl st 1

Fasten off. Leave long tail for sewing.

There are two fins: one long for the top of the tail and one short for the bottom. The half double crochet stitches form the bulge in the middle of the fins.

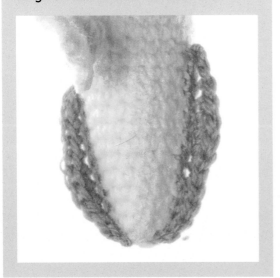

Left Limbs Make 2

R1 With A, sc 4 in magic ring (4)
R2 (sc 1, inc) two times (6)
R3 sc in each st around (6)

Lightly stuff the limb. Pinch sides of the work together. Each sc in **R4** will be made into a matching front and back stitch.

R4 Into front and back stitches, sc 3. These will be referred to as the limb stitches.

The following row will form the toes.

R5 ch 2, skip first ch from hook, sc 1, sc 1 into limb stitch, ch 3, skip first ch from hook, sc 2, sc 1 into limb st, ch 3, skip first ch from hook, sc 2, sl st 1 into limb st

Fasten off. Leave long tail for sewing.

Right Limbs Make 2

R1-4 are the same as the left limbs.

R5 ch 3, skip first ch from hook, sc 2, sc 1 into limb st, ch 3, skip first ch from hook, sc 2, sc 1 into limb st, ch 2, skip first ch from hook, sc 1, sl st 1 into limb st

Fasten off. Leave long tail for sewing.

In row 4, the three limb stitches are made by crocheting into both the front and back stitches. This finishes the rounds.

The left limbs and right limbs are made different by changing row 5.

The tail, body and head are created in separate pieces. This helps form ridges between the sections, although sewing them together gives the look of a continuous head, body and tail.

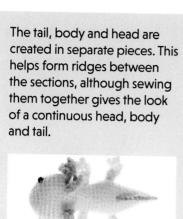

Gill frills are made in one row around a foundation chain.

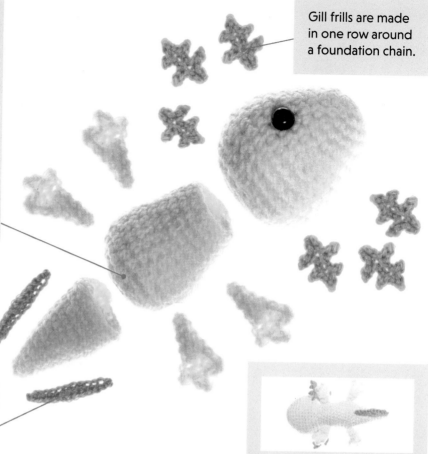

Half double crochet stitches add more width to the middle of the fins.

Fennec Fox

Vulpes zerda

Yarn Colors
Brown (A)
Cream (B)
Black (C)

Notions
2 safety eyes
Stuffing
Black felt

Measurements

11 cm
6 cm
20 cm

Skill Level ● ● ●

Head

R1	With B, sc 6 in magic ring (6)
R2	(sc 1, inc) three times (9)
R3	(sc 2, inc) three times (12)
R4	(sc 1, inc) six times (18)
R5	sc in each st around (18)
R6	(sc 2, inc) six times (24)
R7	Switch to A, (sc 3, inc) two times, switch to B, (sc 3, inc) two times, switch to A, (sc 3, inc) two times (30)
R8	(sc 4, inc) two times, switch to B, (sc 4, inc) two times, switch to A, (sc 4, inc) two times (36)
R9	sc 14, switch to B, sc 8, switch to A, sc 14 (36)
R10	sc 16, switch to B, sc 4, switch to A, sc 16 (36)
R11	sc in each st around (36)
R12	(sc 4, dec) six times (30)
R13	sc in each st around (30)

Cut felt (see template on page 64). Insert safety eyes through felt and onto head. Embroider the nose with C.

R14	(sc 3, dec) six times (24)
R15	(sc 2, dec) six times (18)
R16	(sc 1, dec) six times (12)
R17	dec six times (6)

Finish with a sl st. Leave short tail and weave in.

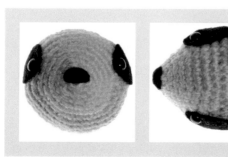

Inner Ears Make 2

R1	With B, sc 6 in magic ring (6)
R2	[sc 3] in next st, inc, [sc 1, hdc 2] in next st, [hdc 2, sc 1] in next st, inc, [sc 3] in next st (16)
R3	sc 1, inc, sc 4, [sc 1, hdc 1] in next st, hdc 2, [hdc 1, sc 1] in next st, sc 4, inc, sc 1 (20)
R4	sc 9, [hdc 1, dc 1] in next st, [dc 1, hdc 1] in next st, sc 9 (22)

Finish with a sl st. Leave short tail and weave in.

Outer Ears Make 2

R1	With A, sc 6 in magic ring (6)
R2	[sc 3] in next st, inc, [sc 1, hdc 2] in next st, [hdc 2, sc 1] in next st, inc, [sc 3] in next st (16)
R3	sc 1, inc, sc 4, [sc 1, hdc 1] in next st, hdc 2, [hdc 1, sc 1] in next st, sc 4, inc, sc 1 (20)
R4	sc 9, [hdc 1, dc 1] in next st, [dc 1, hdc 1] in next st, sc 9 (22)

Lay inner ear piece over the outer ear with the wrong sides facing together. For the following row, crochet into both pieces.

R5	sc 1, inc, sc 8, [hdc 1, dc 1] in next st, [dc 1, hdc 1] in next st, sc 8, sc 1 (26)

Finish with a sl st. Leave long tail for sewing.

Fennec foxes have large ears that radiate heat. This helps them stay cool in the desert.

Body

R1	With A, sc 6 in magic ring (6)
R2	sc 1, [sc 3] four times, sc 1 (14)
R3	sc 5, inc, sc 2, inc, sc 5 (16)
R4	(sc 3, inc) four times (20)
R5	(sc 4, inc) four times (24)
R6-7	sc in each st around (24)
R8	(sc 4, dec) four times (20)
R9	sc 7, dec, sc 2, dec, sc 7 (18)
R10	sc in each st around (18)
R11	(sc 7, dec) two times (16)
R12	(sc 6, dec) two times (14)

Finish with a sl st. Leave long tail for sewing.

Belly

This piece is worked in rows. With B, chain 5.

R1	Skip first ch from hook, sc 4, ch 1 and turn
R2	Skip first ch from hook, sc 1, inc, sc 2, ch 1 and turn
R3	Skip first ch from hook, sc 2, inc, sc 2, ch 1 and turn
R4-5	Skip first ch from hook, sc 6, ch 1 and turn
R6	Skip first ch from hook, dec three times

Crocheting along the edge, sc 16.

Finish with a sl st. Leave long tail for sewing.

Front Legs Make 2

R1	With B, sc 6 in magic ring (6)
R2	inc in each st around (12)
R3	sc 3, (puff st, sc 1) three times, sc 3 (12)
R4	sc 3, dec three times, sc 3 (9)
R5	sc 3, dec, sc 4 (8)
R6	Switch to A, sc in each st around (8)
R7-9	sc in each st around (8)

Finish with a sl st. Leave long tail for sewing.

Thighs Make 2

R1	With A, sc 7 in magic ring (7)
R2	inc three times, [hdc 2], inc three times (14)
R3	sc in each st around (14)

Finish with a sl st. Leave long tail for sewing.

Hind Feet Make 2

R1	With B, sc 6 in magic ring (6)
R2	inc in each st around (12)
R3	sc 3, (puff st, sc 1) three times, sc 3 (12)
R4	sc 4, dec, dec, sc 4 (10)

Finish with a sl st. Leave long tail for sewing.

Tail

R1	With A, sc 5 in magic ring (5)
R2	sc 2, inc, sc 2 (6)
R3	(sc 2, inc) two times (8)
R4-5	sc in each st around (8)
R6	(sc 2, dec) two times (6)
R7	sc in each st around (6)

Cut 15 cm strands of black and beige yarn.

Using the latch hook stitch (see page 14), attach two rows of black yarn strands at the tip of the tail, and attach beige yarn strands onto the rest of the tail. Brush the yarn to create a fluffy tail.

Attach darker strands to the tip of the tail (b) and lighter strands to the base of the tail (c). Brush out the yarn (d).

The inner and outer ear are the same, and they are attached with brown yarn.

The thighs are simple discs that add definition to the rear feet. Stuff and sew onto the body, and attach rear legs to thighs.

Sew belly onto the body before sewing on the legs.

See page 64 for felt template.

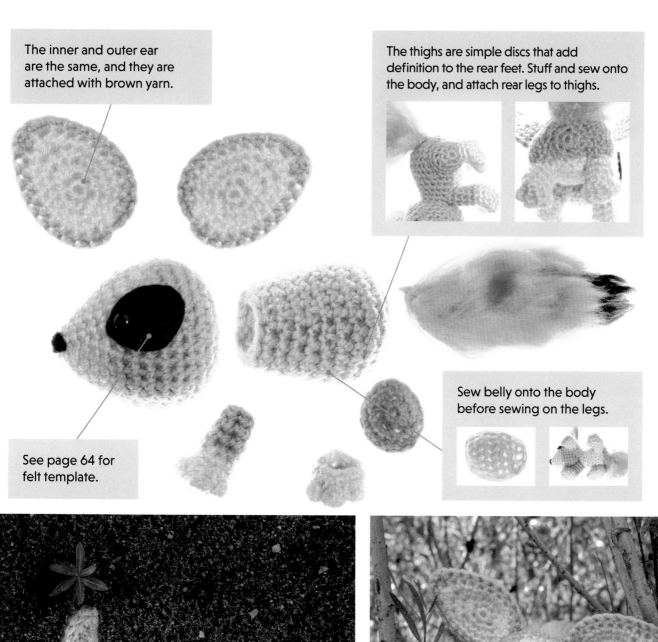

Red Panda

Ailurus fulgens

Yarn Colors
Red (A)
Brown (B)
White (C)
Black (D)

Notions
2 safety eyes
Stuffing
White felt

Measurements

10 cm
8 cm
18 cm

Skill Level ●●○

Head

R1	With A, sc 8 in magic ring (8)
R2	sc 1, inc six times, sc 1 (14)
R3	sc 1, (sc 1, inc) six times, sc 1 (20)
R4	(sc 4, inc) four times (24)
R5	(sc 5, inc) four times (28)
R6	(sc 6, inc) four times (32)
R7-10	sc in each st around (32)
R11	sc 8, inc, inc, sc 12, inc, inc, sc 8 (36)
R12-13	sc in each st around (36)
R14	(sc 4, dec) six times (30)
R15	(sc 3, dec) six times (24)
R16	(sc 2, dec) six times (18)
R17	(sc 1, dec) six times (12)
R18	dec six times (6)

Finish with a sl st. Leave short tail and weave in.

Insert safety eyes.

Muzzle

R1	With C, sc 6 in magic ring (6)
R2	inc, inc, sc 2, inc, inc (10)
R3	(sc 1, inc) five times (15)
R4	sc 6, inc, sc 1, inc, sc 6 (17)

Finish with a sl st. Leave long tail for sewing.

Embroider nose with D.

Cheek Spots Make 2

With C, chain 6.

R1	Skip first ch from hook, sc 1, hdc 1, [hdc 2], hdc 1, sc 1

Fasten off. Leave long tail for sewing.

Eyebrow Spots Make 2

With C, chain 3.

R1	Skip first ch from hook, sc 1, inc

Fasten off. Leave long tail for sewing.

Ears Make 2

R1	With B, sc 6 in magic ring (6)
R2	(sc 1, inc) three times (9)
R3	(sc 2, inc) three times (12)
R4	(sc 3, inc) three times (15)
R5	(sc 4, inc) three times (18)

Finish with a sl st. Leave long tail for sewing.

Cut felt (see page 64 for template) and glue onto ears.

Red pandas can camouflage in fir trees that are covered in a reddish-brown moss.

Body

R1	With A, sc 8 in magic ring (8)
R2	sc 1, inc six times, sc 1 (14)
R3	sc 2, [sc 3] two times, sc 6, [sc 3] two times, sc 2 (22)
R4	sc 3, inc, inc, sc 2, inc, sc 6, inc, sc 2, inc, inc, sc 3 (28)
R5	(sc 6, inc) four times (32)
R6-7	sc in each st around (32)
R8	sc 4, dec, sc 20, dec, sc 4 (30)
R9-10	sc in each st around (30)
R11	sc 12, dec, sc 2, dec, sc 12 (28)
R12	(sc 5, dec) four times (24)
R13-15	sc in each st around (24)
R16	sc 9, dec, sc 2, dec, sc 9 (22)

Finish with a sl st. Leave long tail for sewing.

Front Legs Make 2

R1	With B, sc 8 in magic ring (8)
R2	inc in each st around (16)
R3	sc 5, (puff st, sc 1) three times, sc 5 (16)
R4	(sc 6, dec) two times (14)
R5-6	sc in each st around (14)
R7	(sc 5, dec) two times (12)

Finish with a sl st. Leave long tail for sewing.

Hind Legs Make 2

R1	With B, sc 8 in magic ring (8)
R2	inc in each st around (16)
R3	sc 5, (puff st, sc 1) three times, sc 5 (16)
R4	(sc 6, dec) two times (14)
R5-8	sc in each st around (14)

Finish with a sl st. Leave long tail for sewing.

Tail

R1	With B, sc 6 in magic ring (6)
R2	inc in each st around (12)
R3	(sc 1, inc) six times (18)
R4	sc in each st around (18)
R5	(sc 4, dec) three times (15)
R6	sc in each st around (15)
R7	Switch to A, sc in each st around (15)
R8	sc in each st around (15)
R9	sc 7, dec, sc 6 (14)
R10	Switch to B, sc in each st around (14)
R11	dec, sc 10, dec (12)
R12	Switch to A, sc in each st around (12)
R13	sc in each st around (12)
R14	Switch to B, (sc 4, dec) two times (10)

Finish with a sl st. Leave long tail for sewing.

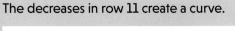

The decreases in row 11 create a curve.

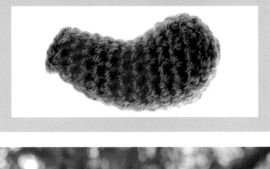

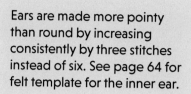

Ears are made more pointy than round by increasing consistently by three stitches instead of six. See page 64 for felt template for the inner ear.

Compared to the front legs, the hind legs are a bit wider at the top.

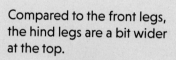

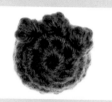

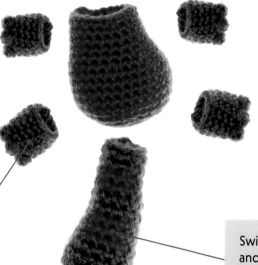

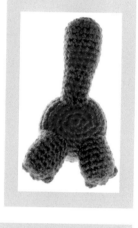

Switching between brown and red create the stripes in the tail.

Felt templates

River Otter Make 2

Page 28

Grey Bat Make 2

Page 32

Raven Make 2

Page 44

Fennec Fox Make 2

Page 56

Red Panda Make 2

Page 60

Phillip Ha is a teacher and amigurumi artist from Calgary, Alberta. Follow his latest creations at www.sirpurlgrey.com or @sirpurlgrey on Instagram.

Jeff Wiehler is a writer and communications specialist from Calgary, Alberta. His writings and pictures are at www.jeffwiehler.com and @jeffwiehler on Instagram.

Thanks to our friends, family and colleagues for their support throughout this entire project.

Made in the USA
Middletown, DE
07 September 2017